Copyright © 2021 Anna Elizabeth Judd All Rights Reserved

All Rights Reserved. No part of this publication may be reproduced or transmitted in any form or by any means, mechanical or electronic, including photocopying and recording, or by any information storage and retrieval system, without permission in writing from the author or publisher (except by a reviewer, who may quote brief passages and/or show brief video clips in a review).

Disclaimer: The Publisher and the Author make no representation or warranties concerning the accuracy or completeness of the contents of this work and specifically disclaim all warranties for a particular purpose. No warranty may be created or extended through sales or promotional materials. The advice and strategies contained herein may not be suitable for every situation. This work is sold with the understanding that the Author and Publisher are not engaged in rendering legal, technological, or other professional services. If professional assistance is required, the services of a competent professional should be sought. Neither the Publisher nor the Author shall be liable for damages arising therefrom.

The fact that an organization or website is referred to in this work as a citation and/or potential source of further information does not mean that the Author or the Publisher endorses the information, the organization, or website it may provide, or recommendations it may make. Further, readers should be aware that the websites listed in this work may have changed or disappeared between when this work was written and when it is read. Disclaimer: The cases and stories in this book have had details changed to preserve privacy.

ISBN Paperback: 978-1-64873-199-0

Printed in the United States of America

Published by: Writer's Publishing House
writerspublishinghouse.com
Prescott, Az 86301

Project Management and Book Launch by Writers Publishing House

Cover and Interior Design by Creative Artistic Excellence Marketing: lizzymcnett.com

The Power of Thought
By Anna Elizabeth Judd

PREFACE

My passions have always dwelt within assisting others in one form or fashion. As a young child, I grew up raising and training horses. The main thing I learned was the art of perfection: We may never truly reach flawlessness, but we must strive for that result each day.

Years ago, I discovered a book called, *The Science of Getting Rich* and it transformed everything in my life. As my pursuit of success continued, I found another author, Catherine Ponder, who wrote the series *The Secrets of Prosperity*, and again it enlightened a new way of thought.

The messages started quite simple and then progressed into more detailed examples for anyone to comprehend the meaning. They changed everything; the world, and life in general. I understood my mistakes and why things were stagnated. It was time for a change.

The lessons exceeded my expectations, and doors opened a great ghostwriting career for clients worldwide. Take a chance and move forward with your life assignments, you only risk success when you stop dreaming.

TABLE OF CONTENTS

Preface ___ 3
Introduction ___ 5
The Power of Thought ___ 7
Materialize as your dreams: ___ 10
Initializing Your Dreams ___ 16
The Brain Game ___ 17
The Delete Button ___ 24
Brain Power ___ 28
Distractions ___ 35
Brain Behavior ___ 41
Think Your Way to Success ___ 47
Grow Your Wealth ___ 49
Reap the Rewards ___ 52
Author Bio ___ 56

INTRODUCTION

Today is your day?

> "The Best Way to Predict Your Future is Create it," President Lincoln.

What do you have to lose, after all, your past is just a snapshot of the former days--the latter is yet to come? The future is a blank canvas, so go ahead and create the life you desire.

Imagination is a powerful tool, existing at everyone's fingertips. It is better to aim high and miss than aim low and hit. If you don't aim at anything, you won't hit anything. My question here is: What are you going to do with the rest of your life?

Decide right now to not let anything stop you. Begin to rid yourself of the negative thoughts from your mind. The only thing that will stop you is, well, YOU! We are each given one destiny and one life. We are given the chance to put things in place and create a plan, to overcome every obstacle!

Go ahead and hire yourself as a chief operator. The best is yet to come! Learn the art of intelligent communication, like never before. The power of words will bring a voice to your potential, and the law of attraction draws the tools necessary to build the ultimate victory!

THE POWER OF THOUGHT

The power of thought is an incredible innate genetic tool all humans possess. The key is learning to unlock its potential. As you read the pages from this book, the intent is to equip each person with the desire to dominate their dreams.

Once you acquire the realization of how your thoughts can create wealth it's game over. Success is emanated; you can turn what you love to do into money.

We are all leaders in some shape form or fashion. My question is, are you leading or just talking a walk? If no one is following, then check the path you are pursuing.

People want to follow leaders. In the 21st century, humans seek new methods and techniques to overcome the challenges of life.

Leaders study research and learn how to maximize their unique gifts in such a way that success is the only outcome. The results allow them to live the American dream.

There is some confusion about what the American dream represents. Misconceptions are owning a fancy house and buying lots of tangible items. All of those things are fantastic goals, but the ultimate target should be waking up every morning doing what you love. Hence, a successful entrepreneur lives life on his or her terms and dictates their worth. No one tells them when to clock in for work, what days two days a week they have off, and most important that person's worth is not decreed by how much they make an hour for someone else's accomplishments.

The power of thought begins with your ability to tap the genetic material you possess. Look inside yourself and ask this priceless question. What is my genetically designed purpose, the one thing I execute with ease? I can perform with precision. Then, focus on how can you maximize this life assignment?

My instructions start by creating a powerful and dominant mental mindset that will allow you to focus and concentrate on your purpose. You should be so focused on what you were born to do others wonder whether you are possessed or obsessed with reaching your dreams and goals. It is after you reach this level of concentration that your innate desires surface and success becomes real.

I mentor, and coach talented writers every day, and being able to use what I've been gifted to do has allowed these individuals to give birth to their dreams. Each day I strive to accomplish my visions in every area of life.

My motto is: "You get strength by helping others succeed. Books are the creators of knowledge."

I want to share my bulletproof formula that has helped people around the country tap into their life assignments. This method of Purpose, Passion, and Power is designed to impact and empower you with the tools and resources you will need to maximize your potential.

MATERIALIZE AS YOUR DREAMS:

Initially, you must obtain a clear picture of what you want by visually seeing your dreams and goals on the plasma screen of your mind; whatever it is you want to accomplish as a leader. Then, push rewind from this picture. Brian Tracy called it back from the future. It is at this point; you become so focused on the result that the challenges you will face during the process do not hinder you from reaching your goals. When you reach this phase of your journey, everything becomes easy. The puzzle pieces align perfectly. You literally eat, sleep and breathe your life assignment.

When you visually connect with something, a force field ignites the passion within. Once you light the fuel, it gives you the power to launch your destiny. The alignment connects you to a place filled with wealth and providence.

Purpose - In the past others have created the path you walk. The individuals reap the benefits of your labor. You are left to wonder when is it my turn to take to lead. When you become a visionary, you will take control.

Start with Purpose –

> ➤ What are you purposed to do in life?

- What is your innate gift to humanity?
- The one thing you master with confidence?

What is that one thing or one area in your life you find yourself doing even when you don't have to?

The one thing you would do without getting paid?

People comment on your ability to perform certain tasks without thought or struggle. The process becomes second nature.

The answer is simple: Life assignment.

Develop this area of expertise. Discipline your mind to function this skill without any thought. Demonstrate your skills to the world. Dominate in your field of specialization. It is your power place as Les Brown would call it. This is your place and space in the universe. Your DNA – Dynamic Natural Ability.

Passion - Passion is the fire from within that fuels your emotions, thus allowing one to move to action. Supercharge your emotions by becoming energized each day. Take charge by listening to audio Mp3 and reading books that will stimulate your inner being in a positive fashion. Your attitude is the most powerful weapon that you have.

Your mind is the control tower of who you are. Everything you do begins with your thought process. Imagine the power you have in your mind. Success creates itself when your focus streamlines on the vision of your victory. Whether right or wrong, it all starts with your mental mindset.

Start every morning and go to bed every night with powerful positive thoughts being rehearsed over and over and over until it seizes your subconscious. It is powerful when you become so disciplined every thought in your mind focuses on how you can make this world a better place because you have birthed your dreams.

It's called the Purposeful Power Zone.

Power – Power is the direct result of every element is fully charged to accomplish your dreams and goals. The level of power you possess determines the elements, energy, and the amount of force you put into packaging your desired explosive personal powerbomb.

The eruption exposes overflowing abundance in your life. Wealth beyond your wildest dreams flows from every direction. Peace settles deep; nothing can phase the joy and most of all you feel an increasing desire to help guide those brought into your path. The guidance is carried out with no expectations, just willingness to show others how they can achieve their Purposeful Power Zone.

The obsession begins to infect family members, friends, and loved ones of all areas far and wide. A person who shares the power of thought spreads the infectious behavior, enabling others to reap what they sow.

One word of caution: Disclosing your dreams and plans with people who don't share your optimism may lead to false insight. The important factor is communicating this powerful purpose technique with any human whenever the situation provides. Granting access to your path must be restricted to the people of your inner circle.

Many individuals find meditation or quiet times during the day create incredible results. Once you learn to become one with the universe and open your mind to endless possibilities your life assignment will visualize loud and clear. These results will allow you to become a driving force within your personal and professional life.

Many people are unaware the methods they were taught are to help someone else to succeed. This book will help you to understand the basics of tapping into your natural talents and how to alter your thoughts and begin creating new wealth for yourself.

What does that mean? We are granted an education at a young age to build essential skills for survival in society. Then, move forward to developing an expertise in a field serving someone else. In other words, go to work.

Let someone else identify your talents in an interview, hire you, then incorporate your efforts to assist them in becoming wealthy. Don't get me wrong; it's great to grow up and allow corporate America to pay you a salary that in return allows you to live a certain quality of life. My question is what quality of life are they allowing you to live?

These excellent techniques over the years worked well in the industrial industries when the occupation or position you held defined the person inside. Society is moving solely into the information era, traveling at the speed of thought. The industrial industry is becoming a thing of the past. Free enterprise is dominating the world. The reign allows individuals to turn what they love to do into wealth.

In other words, the next generation has already made a conscious decision they are not going to work for someone or the same company for twenty or thirty years, retire, get a gold watch, and two years later have a heart attack, stroke, and die; never being able to fulfill their destiny or life assignment.

As you look forward to becoming the dynamic leader, you are capable of being, it is important to know the leader on the outside is manifested from the leader on the inside.

Purpose is what you were created to become. Passion is what guides you to that Purpose. Power is what you need to fuel and ignite the Plan. By maximizing your innate potential, you will take ownership and become the leader others will follow.

INITIALIZING YOUR DREAMS

"Leader of one, Leader of many. If you can't lead one, then you can't lead any." - unknown

THE BRAIN GAME

Often the brain is described as being "like a muscle." It is a rule of education that keeps school children hunched over their desks. We judge literacy and numeracy exercises as more beneficial for intelligence than running, playing, and learning on the move. But the analogy does not work. To build up your biceps, you cannot avoid flexing them. When it comes to your brain, an oblique approach is surprisingly effective. Working your body's muscles will benefit your grey matter. Scientists have shown that a runners' euphoric high and the tranquility found in yoga have profound effects. Moreover, specific physical activities markedly alter its structure in precise ways.

A wave of studies exploring the unexpected links between cerebral and bodily fitness is emerging from labs. The research gives impetus to become more active. It may also help you choose the best options to prepare physically for mental challenges such as exams, interviews, and creative projects.

Boost Your Memory

The hippocampus reacts strongly toward aerobic exercise. Controlled experiments in children, adults, and the elderly show this structure grows as people get fitter. Since the hippocampus is at the core of the brain's learning and memory systems, this finding partly explains the memory-boosting effects of improved cardiovascular fitness. Also, slowly improving your retention hardware, exercise may have a more immediate impact on memory formation. Researchers showed that walking or cycling during, but not before, assisted in learning a new foreign language, so exercise while you revise. Don't push too hard though. Vigorous workouts raise your stress levels, which can scupper recollection circuits.

Improve Concentration

Besides making memories stickier, exercises may help you focus and stay on task. The best scientific evidence comes from testing school children, but the same applies likely to us all. Interspersing lessons with 20-minute bouts of aerobics-style isometrics improved the attention spans of students. Meanwhile, a large randomized controlled trial looked at the effects of daily extracurricular sports classes over one year. The students, of course, became fitter. But more importantly, their ability to ignore distractions improved, along with, maintaining their lessons increased dramatically. Research shows just ten minutes a day will improve attention span and intelligence of anyone.

Improve Mental Health

Love it or hate it, bouts of physical activity can have potential effects on your mood. The runner's high, that feeling of elation following intense exercise, is real. Even mice get it. It may not be due to an "endorphin rush" however. Levels of the body's homemade opiate do rise in the bloodstream, but it is not clear how much endorphin gets into the brain. Instead, recent evidence points to a pleasurable and painkilling firing of the endocannabinoid system: the psychoactive receptor of cannabis.

Anxiety Debilitates Learning

When anxiety levels rise, you tense up, your heart races and attention diminishes. The "fight or flight" mode is automatic, but that does not mean it is wholly out of your control. Yoga teaches the deliberate command of movement and breathing, intending to turn on the body's "relaxation response". Science increasingly backs this claim. For example, a 2010 study put participants through eight weeks of daily stretching meditation practice. The results were amazing. Brain scans showed a reduction, shrinkage in part of their amygdala, a deep structure strongly implicated in processing stress, fear, and anxiety.

Workouts are also emerging as a promising way to overcome depression. A 2013 meta-analysis cautiously reported that exercise – both aerobic and resistance – was "moderately effective" in treating depressive symptoms. (PHD, n.d.)   Strikingly, the results were equal to that of anti-depressant drugs and psychological treatments. The author's study identified it as an area crying out for rigorous investigation.

Enhance Creativity

Thoreau Nietzsche and many other creative minds claim walking gives wings to the imagination. Last year, psychologists gave this empirical support. Walking, either on a treadmill or down a sunny beach, bolstered divergent thinking or the free-roaming, idea-generating component of creative thought.

Slowing Cognitive Decay

The evidence that staying physically fit keeps your brain healthy through to your advanced years is especially compelling. Most detailed studies link aerobic fitness and cognitive preservation. Workouts need not be extreme either. Thirty to forty-five minutes of brisk walking, three times a week, can help fend off the mental wear and tear and delay the onset of dementia. Though you can reap the benefits of regular exercise early. The protective effects are clearest before the cognitive signs of old age.

It is not all about your heart and lungs. Exercises to improve balance, coordination and agility made a clear impact on the brain structure and cognitive function of a large group of older adults. Twice weekly sessions of weightlifting can have visible neurological results. Dancing may also be restorative for aging brains. Just an hour of dance a week, for six months, bolstered their physical and social well-being.

Researchers are still testing the critical factors that make exercise such a potent brain tonic. Prime suspects include increased blood flow to the brain, surges of growth hormones, and expansion of the brain's network of blood vessels. It's also possible that workouts stimulate the birth of new neurons. Until recently, few believed this could happen in the adult human.

Exercise Regularly

The cognitive spillover reminds us that we don't operate in isolation. What you do with your body impinges on your mental faculties. Sitting stagnant is dangerous, so, don't dither about the type of exercise. Find a training program and stick with the plan.

The Deliberate Brainwork is a guide to overcome your negative thinking and conditioned state of mind; to challenge your limiting beliefs. Many people live on 'autopilot' in a negative conditioned state, unsatisfied and miserable.

Learn to alter your way of thinking, by prioritizing your goals and plans. The thought should follow your professional and personal life. What do you have to lose?

Gain clarity by living your life with purpose, rather than following a crowd. It's about becoming who you want to be and reaching your potential.

The following are common effects of modern living that have an adverse effect, often leading to anxiety, stress, and unhappiness in both our professional and personal lives.

> ➢ Procrastination or being stuck.
> ➢ Self-doubt or thinking you're not good/smart enough to be successful.
> ➢ Loss of focus and direction.
> ➢ Feelings of overwhelm or confusion about how to change.
> ➢ Scared of making mistakes and being a failure.

The initial step to overcome the effects begins with prioritizing your goals. Start gradually, one day at a time. Sometimes, we get caught up in the chaos, and our vision is muffled. Therefore, we lose sight of the big picture. At that point, negativity settles, and hopes vanish. We start to justify the failures, walking away from our life assignments.

THE DELETE BUTTON

Neuroscience has a saying,

> "Neurons that fire together wire together."

The more you run a neuro-circuit in your brain, the stronger that path becomes. Therefore, to quote another old saw, practice makes perfect. The neural links reinforce.

The study of education is about building and strengthening neural connections. The focus cannot be on just cramming in new data. If the links are weak, retention of the material will not last. Our brain gives us the ability to break down old connections and create stronger paths, called "synaptic pruning."

Your Brain Is Like a Garden

The connections in your brain resemble a garden. Plants are growing and multiplying through synaptic connections that run between neurons. The brain has connections called neurotransmitters. These function from dopamine, serotonin, and others they travel across. The "glial cells" have multiple functions; they are gardeners which work to speed up signals between certain neurons. The other job is waste removal, pulling up weeds, killing pests, or raking up dead leaves. Your brain's pruning shears are called, "microglial cells." They clean your synaptic connections.

Researchers are just starting to unravel this mystery, but what they do know is the synaptic connections (memories/thoughts/ideas) used the least and got marked by a protein, C1q (as well as others). When the microglial cells detect that mark, they bond to the protein and destroy– or prune–the synapse. That is how your brain makes the physical space to build new and stronger connections so you can learn more.

Why Sleep Matters

As the day progresses and you are actively living life, your brain gets full. The space in your head overflows and pushes against your skull to make room. If you don't sleep enough, the available space fills quickly. Even though you are always taking in new information, the area is cramped. When you learn new things, the brain builds links, but they're inefficient ad-hoc connections. For your brain to develop efficient pathways, it must prune the associations. The cleaning process happens when you sleep-- your brain cells shrink up to 60% allowing for space, while the glial gardeners come to take away the waste and prune the synapses.

A full nights' rest will leave you thinking clearly. The pruning freed the pathway, leaving room to synthesize new information: In other words, to learn.

A sleep-deprived brain is like hacking your way through a dense jungle with a machete. It's overgrown, slow-going, exhausting. The paths overlap, and light cannot get through.

The well-rested mind would be as if you are wandering along a beach with the gentle waves caressing the shoreline; the paths are clear and connect at distinct spots, everything is in place, and you communicate accurately. It's invigorating.

The same concept applies to naps. A ten or twenty-minute rest gives your microglial gardeners the chance to come in, clear away some unused connections, and leave space to grow new ones.

Thoughts Produce Change

In fact, thoughts can change your memories scientifically. Any synaptic connection you don't use is earmarked for recycling. When you sleep, the brain decides what to throw away or keep, hence omit the bad thoughts and memories with new fresh ideas.

The concept makes it imperative to be cautious of what you say and think. Your focus becomes your reality. Essentially, you are the product of your thoughts.

If you spend your time contemplating negative thoughts, the results of everything around you will be destructive. Success will evade your every path, not only mentally but physically.

To take advantage of your brain's natural gardening system, simply think about the things that are important to you. Your gardeners will strengthen those connections and prune the ones that you care about less. It's how you help the garden of your brain flower.

BRAINPOWER

In this chapter, I will discuss living in the present and not the past. It is the first step in dealing with bad habits. These interrupt our lives and prevent us from achieving greatness. Negativity not only jeopardizes your health--both mentally and physically--it is a waste of time and energy. Ask yourself, why am I hanging onto a plague when I can swap it with healthy successful practices.

I do not possess all the answers, but if you keep reading, I share my knowledge and experience. Constructive methods come from learning to reduce tension or monotony. Unpleasant days occur, but they are only temporary.

Habits often appear from deeper issues. Stress and boredom are just residual effects. These problems are tough to acknowledge, but change requires commitment. Be honest with yourself.

Individual beliefs bring these practices to the surface without the person's conscious understanding. Some results about fear, or anxiety often produce debilitating effects.

Overcome Undesired Behavior

The only option to eliminate unwanted action is to replace it with healthy behaviors. Habits emerge for a reason, and the routine may worsen without mannerism. The benefit provided comfort.

For instance; smoking or drugs, the practice arose due to an emotional situation, relationship problems with family, or a domestic partner. Your customs are formed to cope with stress.
The source stimulated the action.

One example: The urge to maintain a constant connection with your technological device is in the middle of everyone's life. It is an avoidance practice to ignore real issues. The habit surfaces divide your attention and destroy productivity. (Therefore, simplistic advice like, "just stop doing it" rarely works). The feelings remain dominant, so ignoring them won't diffuse their strength.

Here is an instance where going cold turkey could cause additional hardships. If smoking is used to relieve anxiety, you might turn to other unhealthy options to fill the void. Find an outlet for the stress that has proven effects on your mental and physical well-being. One incredible option, exercise. Small amounts each day can foster positive results. The alternate choice is personal, but be certain it's healthy.

Break a Bad Habit

The first step is commitment and a desire to transform your life. It may seem obvious, but understanding the reason behind the behavior is imperative to achieving success.

People embark on change without certainty it's what they want. Breaking habits can be difficult; you must prepare. Most habitual behaviors are patterns that evolved because we're rewarded. They make it easier to perform a common task or to deal with various emotional states.

We fall into a "habit loop." The trigger tells your brain when to start the expected behavior. A reward is processed for this mannerism, in the form of neurochemicals, which reinforces the unyielding circle. By interrupting the pattern, it initiates change. Examine the context; decide the most efficient way to break the action. It will be helpful to determine the emotional triggers, which control the brain's reward center. The knowledge allows you to develop a beneficial understanding means of achieving the same rewards of the habit provided.

The rituals emerged from dealing with conditions of stress or boredom.

For example: For most people, smoking delivers relief from hectic situations. Procrastination provides freedom to engage in fun activities.

When you feel the sensation to perform your habitual action, make a note of it. Often, practices become ingrained; we don't even notice why we do them. By developing that awareness, you can pinpoint what is happening to prompt your routine.

By creating a post-it, can trigger your brain into altering its behavior and stop the urge to engage in this type of activity.

For example: If you are a nail-biter, note whenever you get the impulse to bite your nails. Notate the circumstances when you felt the cravings.

Make a Plan

Once you understand the causes, set a goal to replace the behavior with strategies for minimizing the habit. Studies show having a specific design increases your chance of success. It helps break down unwanted behaviors and creates new patterns of action.

Plan Mistakes

Do not create a strategy deemed to failure because of a single slip-up. Many of us give in to temptation. If you accept this in advance, you may not let negativity defeat the whole enterprise. Be careful not to justify your actions and use them as an excuse to quit. We learn from our errors. You should include mechanisms for keeping yourself accountable, in the form of rewards for successes and feedback from others who support your goal. You are more likely to succeed if you share the plan.

Visualize Success

In your mind, imagine the day when the undesired practice no longer controls your life. When you anticipate a situation, success will be easier. It helps reinforce positive, productive patterns.

For example: If your goal is to eat less junk food, create healthy meal plans and snacks. Use the internet for alternative actions that lead to your success. Talk to people who have achieved the desired result. But, make it fun.

A major stride in breaking habits is understanding how your brain learns. Humans absorb new things through practice and repetition. What I mean is, study the lesson, become familiar with all the topics, then speak with a professional or successful person you want to emulate. By teaching others, the brain interprets the action as an important subject and creates pathways to deal with the situation. If you forget a step and get lost, simply restudy the section and try again.

Mindful Diligence

Daily life can become monotonous, and we often function on autopilot. The less attentive you are to normal rituals;

gaps open in your plans to alter your behavior. Counteract bad habits with good mannerisms to avoid the circumstance and focus on the end game.

Concentration teaches our brain to react in different ways to certain situations. It can reprogram how you respond to events and stressors. The change allows time to think before you respond, breaking the "automatic pilot." Be conscious of temptations.

- ➢ What triggers lead to unwanted action?
- ➢ What sensations in your body or thoughts promote undesired behavior?

The last precaution to be aware of is likely the most relevant section in this chapter — do not suppress feelings about your habit. Your brain ironically will continuously emit impulses if you ignore a desire.

The concept is avoidance, or a more familiar term is procrastination. and will enhance the situation to make matters worse. The conscious acknowledgment will overcome unwanted behavior. The first step in changing your life is admitting the problem. You are much better off recognizing your craving and the situations that promote it, than deal with these issues head-on.

Meditation

A body and mind that function as one become the embodiment of perfection. When you practice focusing on breathing and calming your mind, you will develop an awareness of your true beliefs.

Yoga and Tai Chi are excellent substitutes for replacing bad behaviors. You are the image of perfection, follow your heart, and you can achieve greatness.

Note, when the habit emerges and draws you to submit, acknowledge the emotion and stop, think before you act. Practice meditation. Your mind is the control tower of who you are. Everything you do begins with your thought process. Imagine the power of the mind. Results dictate the way you perceive the world. Whether it is right or wrong, it starts with your mental mindset. Hard times are inevitable in life, but with the proper tools, anyone can succeed.

DISTRACTIONS

Distraction riddle everyone at a point or another. The important factor is learning how to manipulate the issues; by maintaining interferences, progress will proceed. Once you can gain control, the ability to overcome will prevail. No one can afford disruptions, especially entrepreneurs. Therefore, understanding how to restrain your thoughts and circumstances will help diminish the occurrences.

These pesky little nuisances come in two forms; Internal and External.

External distractions are sometimes out of our control. Diversions are always unforeseen, but the way you handle the situation is the point offered here.

A few examples:

- *Unexpected guest*
- *Phone call from your best friend, or a new love interest*
- *Shopping for non-essential items*
- *Tending to your family*
- *Illness or death of a loved one*
- *Employment responsibilities*

Internal distractions arise from within our mind. Immediate thoughts can often disrupt your plans. When the feelings emerge, they are remnants of a bad habit trying to resurface.

A few examples:

- Excuse for going to the store
- Maintaining a constant connection with social media sites
- A nap due to feeling boredom
- Playing instead of working on your dreams
- Watching TV

Diversions kill success if left uncontrolled. We will discuss some alternatives to minimize their power over your life.

Professionals possess some theories about what internal causes force these distractions to surface.

- Worry of inadequacy
- Boredom searching for your real purpose
- An intimidating project
- Loneliness or Co-dependent
- Uncertainty of an outcome
- Fear of failure

Carefully examine the reason for your conflict, it may not always be a bad instinct. Anytime a gut-wrenching knot is telling you to stop, STOP. The emotion is there for a reason. A crucial key to accomplishing your goals is understanding your mind and body. But, be mindful the resistance is real. A daily schedule can help reduce anxiety and alleviate stress.

Govern External Distractions

There are several options for governing external interruptions.

Plan Ahead: Determine the biggest distractions in your life. Then, order them by priority. If you have a family, take care of their needs first, leaving time to complete your tasks. Or pets; use the same process. The type of interference does not matter, find ways to work around their troublesome effects and move forward.

Handle the Disturbance Quickly: In other words, planning your daily schedule minimizes the distractions. It may even be necessary to incorporate the entire week. Set boundaries, for yourself and your family.

Productive Free Zones: The first task is to secure a peaceful place. A Plan only works in this space, never entertain or socialize. It allows your brain to adjust its yearnings and decrease internal disruptions. Keep focused.

Minimize Internal Distractions

Some other options:

Be the Boss: Internal distractions offer a different set of rules. They require a higher commitment to maintain and overcome. Here are five techniques you can use:

Face the Problems: Unfounded emotions are proven to have developed from fear. In most cases, the fear is about failing. (FEAR) Forget Everything and Run. A silly statement for a ridiculous action. Disappointment is a second chance to start over. It's time to take the bull by the horns, dig deep and learn from your mistakes. Turn bad into good.
Education is always an excellent teacher.

Cure Boredom: Monotony is difficult for all humans, especially since our society predicates instant gratification. A great outlet to reduce stress are self-reward, stimulation to the body and the mind. In the beginning chapters, I discussed exercise. Therefore, the reward must be something to initialize brain function. Eliminate boredom by finding inner peace. In certain circumstances, you may feel trapped because of financial issues, but that is not a reason to do nothing. Excuses are another internal distraction. If this scenario is a reality for you, then partake in the activities while you create enough money to finance your life assignment.

Eliminate Conflict: To discover your purpose means ending unfounded fears or even excuses. The defiance is surfacing for a reason, uncover the issue. The deep-down gut-wrenching nagging won't go away. It can be difficult to face the truth, but reality brings forgiveness.

Inadequate Emotions: You don't have to get it right, just get it going. Many times, our past caused deficient feelings. The unfounded notions. We all encompass a unique purpose, find your life assignment! It is your job to discover that talent. If you walk around afraid, the unique skill will never appear.

The Unknown: A common phobia. We all suffer from the same fears; some are worse than others. You are better off to aim high and miss than aim low and hit. The undetermined future can be alarming, don't let it become debilitating. Overcome and reap the rewards.

When distractions come to plague your life, remember the reason you started this venture. Most people forget why they started something and stop before the magic happens.

Progress takes time and therefore, you must look at the small everyday hurdles. The significant obstacles will take care of themselves. By keeping a journal of your growth patterns, it is easy to stay committed to the end. Finally, be kind to yourself. Success will prevail when you achieve inner peace.

BRAIN BEHAVIOR

Change Your Environment

Life crises can have everlasting effects, and certain situations cause behaviors to compensate for the circumstances. Therefore, by reducing temptation, we help to eliminate negative practices and minimize the triggers that evoke the urge.

Innovative plans of action force us to use our brains and make conscious decisions, rather than slipping into automatic behavioral patterns.

A good way to avoid bad habits is to change the scenery and see if the practice becomes less tempting. For instance, if you like to smoke out on your patio, remove the chair and replace it with a plant. If you overeat at the dining room table, move to an alternate seat or rearrange your furniture. Subtle changes to the environment can minimize the rote and force your mind to reassess what's happening.

One major factor is our regular relationships. Forge other acquaintances with individuals that support your desired behavior. You can keep your old friends, but finding people who live your new lifestyle can lessen triggers.

Change your routine when possible. An efficient way to stop habits is to move to a different situation while developing healthier routines. Afterward, transplant these good attitudes into your normal life when you return.

Create Barriers to the Habit

Fresh obstacles that make the pattern more difficult or unpleasant assist you in breaking the routine.

Here are a few suggestions:

- Tell supportive people about the plan and invite them to call you out on your slip-ups. It will generate consequences for succumbing to temptation.
- Find a successful partner.

Anything to break up the sequence of events leading to undesirable behavior is a good idea.

For example:

- To quit smoking, keep your cigarettes in another room or in an area that would create an inconvenience.
- Limit social media time. Disconnect the internet or use one of the available apps that block access to sites.

Even though you can overcome these obstacles, they are sometimes enough to break up the developed pattern.

Create small "punishments" for lapses.

For example:

> ➢ It is the same rationale as a swear jar when you slip put a dollar in the pot. Set an amount you'll dislike whenever you give in to the urge and stick to it. When you have kicked the habit, spend the money on a reward or donate it to a charitable cause.

If you are trying to stop overeating, add ten minutes to your workout every time you overeat. A punishment related to the behavior should be sufficient.

Start small. Some habits, such as procrastinating, can be difficult to change because the solution seems daunting. Try splitting up your goals into achievable steps. You will get the "reward" of seeing success sooner, and your brain is less likely to resist the goal.

For example:

> ➢ Amend the thought, "I'll stop eating junk food" to buy healthy meals for breakfast.

> Instead of saying "I'll go to the gym more often" make Saturday morning your workout day.

Set small goals to achieve and the ultimate plan will take care of itself. Do not dwell on what you cannot do, rather, what you can start now.

For example:

> Change from, "I will stop procrastinating today," to set a target, to "I will stay focused on my work for 30 minutes."

Buy a daily calendar or planner. Allocate enough time and focus on one task. The span cannot be over 45 minutes and not less than 20. Once you achieve that goal, take a break! Do something fun. The healthiest option is exercise; however, it must be enjoyable.

When you set new schedules, you trick your mind into changing habits. The euphoria is a stimulant for your brain.

Reward Your Successes

Gratification creates habits; It doesn't matter either good or bad. So, the ultimate result must come from excellent behavior. Immediate satisfaction will reveal the most success.

For example:

- If you are in the routine of being late for work, you could buy yourself a cup of gourmet coffee each day you arrive on time, until the reward is no longer needed.

Fill the Void

Replace your old outlook on life with an upbeat and engaging attitude. The key is to have an alternate action when tempted to engage in a negative practice.

For example:

- To quit a difficult habit; such as smoking, create a daily plan from the moment you wake from bedtime. The list must entail activities for when you perform the undesired routine.

By filling the void, you can minimize a backslide. Try to be sure the alternative action isn't annoying or unappealing. Unenjoyable experiences will not stop bad habits.

Be Patient

Operant conditioning learning in which environmental stimuli control behavior. Reward or punishment reinforces the habit.

Conventional wisdom and self-help books have suggested 28 days to form other behaviors. The reality may not be that simple; it could take a year and during which the residual effects will linger.

Even though this process varies between individuals, it's safe to say the first few days are the hardest. Some neuroscientists suggest people go through a "withdrawal" period over a few weeks, as our nervous systems struggle to deal with a change in the chemicals triggering the "reward" centers of our brains.

Stay Kind to Yourself

A single slip does not mean walk away and give- up, no matter how the present situation appears, it's the long-term effects that count.

If you think the goal is difficult, your mind will reinforce the belief you cannot break the habit. But remember, be easy on yourself. Keep striving to victory!

THINK YOUR WAY TO SUCCESS

The understanding of thought vibration will make you a successful and wealthy person. We've all heard people talking about positive or negative vibes. Science has established the concept.

Thoughts travel the universe. The belief is known as [Applied Kinesiology](), which is a scientifically proven fact. When you connect with love, acceptance, and willingness, an aura forms attracting like-minded individuals. The law of attraction. Imagine the impact. Our thought vibrations create an energy field. If you enter a tense and upset room, the emotions spread. Peace develops from within, and humans are attracted to inner joy.

1. Have you ever noticed how certain people experience misfortune over and over again while others enjoy success?
2. What about the times you are in a foul mood, but find someone upbeat and your emotion changes immediately? We are connected, for better or worse.

3. If you want to raise your intellectual state of mind, change the way you think.

Listed below are a few suggestions.

- ➢ Accept responsibility for your life.
- ➢ Examine your beliefs.
- ➢ Replace negative, limiting ideals with positive aspirations.
- ➢ Get a pet!

It may sound odd, but people who own pets tend to have lower stress levels and live longer. Animal therapists even take dogs and cats to hospitals and nursing homes since humans feel less pain when they are with a pet.

- ➢ Meditate to attain a higher level of consciousness.
- ➢ Discover your life assignment.
- ➢ Seek a positive in every situation.
- ➢ Aspire to achieve the things you want.
- ➢ Focus on your health.
- ➢ Be grateful.
- ➢ Write a gratitude list.
- ➢ Have fun!
- ➢ Spend time with people who motivate you,
- ➢ avoid the energy suckers.
- ➢ Help someone with no ulterior motives.
- ➢ Volunteer for an organization.

> Watch movies, read books or listen to music that lifts your spirits.

The bottom line is that I firmly believe in the power of the mind. If one plans twenty minutes a day to meditate and focus on a better life, the changes will be astounding. You will feel calmer, and progress will come quickly. Pay it forward, give out what you want to receive. Faith without Works is Dead!

Grow Your Wealth

Your thoughts are either faithful servants or tyrannical masters--just as you allow them to be. The decision is entirely up to you. Control your mind and control your wealth.

Thoughts will either work with you or against you. They are directed solely by how you feel and think -- not only in your waking hours but when you are asleep. Some of our best mental work is being performed when our conscious mind is at rest, as it is evidenced by the fact that when the morning comes, we find troublesome problems worked out for us during the night--after we had dismissed them from our minds. Otherwise, those same thoughts enslave us to make foolish decisions if we allow them to do so. More than half of the people in the world are slaves of every vagrant thought which may see fit to torment them.

Your mind was created for you to use and function daily through life and not for it to use you. There are very few people who realize the concept and understand the art of managing the mind. The key to the mystery is concentration. Every human has the power to use their mental machine properly. When you have some cerebral work to do, concentrate on the issue alone, you will find the mind will get right to work resolving the problem. Before long, a solution will be present. It pays to be a competent mental engineer.

The person who understands how to run their mental engine knows one important key, there is a limit that should not be crossed. Any machine needs tune-ups and refueling when the gas tank is empty. If the engine is pushed to its limits without proper care, the machine will break down. The difference being a machine runs on physical parts made of metal or plastic which can be easily replaced. Your brain has no replaceable parts; when it breaks, the system damage may be permanent.

Mental control is an art that takes practice, just like learning to ride a bike. No one is born with these skills; we have to make a conscious effort to educate ourselves. One great practice is meditation.

The practice of controlling your thoughts productively. Someone who lays awake at night fretting over problems of the day or morrow is only wearing the engine to extreme levels. Nothing can be resolved from worry, anger, or stress.

The best option for calming the mind or to solve a problem is thinking of something else. Focus on a subject that brings joy and happiness to your life. The concept of trying to drown and the problem only serves to enhance the situation. It is a complete waste of energy. Stop obsessing over the thought—keep your attention on other practices by an effort of will. Any argument to the contrary is an excuse. Practice is the only outlet to resolve the situation. It all goes back to one simple fact, "How bad do you want to change in your life?"

You must accept the concept of change to bring forth new opportunities. It is only when we don't try that the heavy backpack of regret finds its way into our lives. I would rather aim high and miss than aim low and hit. If you don't aim at anything, you won't hit anything. Today is your day, what issues will you overcome to create a better life for yourself and your family?

REAP THE REWARDS

In this chapter, we discuss what thoughts cost you your true purpose. The law of attraction guides success into your path if you believe.

> I quote, "Faith without works is dead."

The first step in prosperity is demanding all that is yours in the universe. When you expect righteousness—you receive abundance. Ask demand—and take!

We are all equal no one is better and merits more than you. Human society has caused these fears due to greed and control of the secret. Step one, develop the confidence and the courage to possess what is rightfully yours.

The concept is referred to as The Law of Attraction. It is nothing new to modern civilization. Some of the wealthiest humans alive and dead reaped the benefits for centuries. However, some deem the universe has limits, and that we must live in poverty to be a good person and fulfill our spiritual obligation. This is a lie! The resolution is to give the knowledge to others. Our abundance is free-flowing and limitless. We are educated in scarcity, only the rich and smart enjoy luxury. The truth changes your thoughts and alters your world. The mind is a powerful tool when learned to use it properly.

Purpose, Passion, and Power
Strong Desire. Confident Expectation.
Courage in Action.

Victory comes from the desire to achieve greatness, no matter the mountain height. You must become obsessed with your success. Living with fear only serves to push the goal out of sight. The plan may sometimes appear impossible and unreachable; these are the time to alter your thoughts. Opposition bears its presence when you are striving to reach your life assignment. Resistance is a positive response to your actions. Doubt is the killer of every law in receiving overflowing abundance. Stop the skepticism.

The final reminder, we must look at our own goals not what someone else finds appealing. Vibrations of the universe revolt instinctively against taking something that is not yours. The mind is honest. It is an innate nature to understand right from wrong. If you have to hide and shun from your actions, it's the subconscious shuttering and recoiling.

A common misconception about attraction is that you can wish your way to wealth. The fact remains there is a difference between belief and strong wishing. Successful people know their ultimate goals and acknowledge setbacks, stumble and create a plan. Failure is seen as an option to start over with a better version of the original idea. The only outcome is victory. I would rather target high and miss than aim low and hit.

Someone who considers failure is sure to fail. There is no special miracle or a hidden switch; you must believe. The concept of quitting never enters their consciousness. Negative ideas stop the minute one tries to break through. Closed minds block creativity. It is only when with enthusiasm and hope that our subconscious works with precision. A prevailing mental attitude succeeds in every course.

The law of attraction operates by the sheer will to prevail; nothing happens by chance. It is as plain as mathematics. Plan and purpose—cause and effect. The fall of the stone down the mountainside by accident—forces which had been in operation for centuries caused it. Copious decrees are in full campaign whether you believe and acknowledge their existence. You must stay within the laws to receive overflowing abundance. An opposition of edicts only brings friction into your life; it doesn't affect the directives in any way.

Again, I say, "Your thoughts are real."

The final point, be cautious of your environment. Our minds attract the brainwaves of others—conscious or unconscious. So, stay alert to the surroundings and how you let people alter your attitude. In time, thought-currents merge with like-minded individuals and conditions in harmony with your note of visions. Paired as one and your purpose will work to assist in each other's prosperity. Get into its flow and maintain your poise. Set your mind to the keynote of Courage, Confidence, and Success: You can expect nothing but the best.

AUTHOR BIO

Anna provides it all as if you are in the saddle along for the journey. Her rare books bring the readers joy from nearly every genre they can appreciate. She exuberantly brings the image and sentiments of the west to full life throughout the storyline. Yet, at the core of Judd's work is a black stallion who engages life into every aspect of the book. Haystack fills children's minds with wonder as he interacts with Marshal Spur and the Outrider Gang, to the mild minored young steed who brings Adam to new levels of learning in his life. Then he is brilliantly portrayed as a beautiful Appaloosa stallion in the Broncobuster as Cash.

Anna is one of the greatest novelists and a freelance ghostwriter is known for equestrian professionalism in every genre. Her young adult fiction novels and all books bring joy to the readers.

Lizzy is the founder of Writers Publishing House/Ghost Writer Media, who writes under her pen name Anna Elizabeth Judd, a solid publishing firm with more than a decade of assisting clients will their publishing needs. She has a BA in fine arts, with a minor in Equine Science. On the side, she studied at Scottsdale Art Institute under Robert 'Shoofly' Shufelt.

Lizzy writes books, which considering this website, makes perfect sense. She is best known for ghostwriting various best sellers in all genres. Along with her novels based on the initial part of her working career, horse training. As she understands the importance of family values, Lizzy chose a pen name borrowed from her family tree, Anna Elizabeth Judd.

When not absorbed in writing for clients, Lizzy can be found hiking, biking, or any outside activity. Although she does not train horses any longer, their spirits will always be a part of her soul. As a passionate entrepreneur Lizzy understands the importance of exemplary customer service, it is the basis for any successful business. In this case, Writers Publishing House was founded on the idea that the focus must be on the client's success. She believes, "Everyone should profit from their passion."

If you want to know more about publishing a book, please visit her website at https://writerspublishinghouse.com where you can contact her about starting your book project today.

Anna's Books: annaelizabethjudd.com

- The Power of Thought
- IAuthor – Social Media Marketing Guide

- The Handbook of Horsemanship
- The Broncobusters
- The Hourglass of el Diablo

- Marshal Spur and the Outlaw
- The Boy Who Couldn't Talk
- Spur Up! – Music Album
- Hey, Hay Learn Your ABC's
- Learn Your ABCs with Haystack

- A Distant Calling
- Skimmer's Adventure

www.ingramcontent.com/pod-product-compliance
Lightning Source LLC
Chambersburg PA
CBHW071916070526
44583CB00016B/2014